D1449879

ANIMAL DANGER ZONE

CROCODILE!

Willow Clark

WINDMILL
BOOKS

New York

Published in 2011 by Windmill Books, LLC
303 Park Avenue South, Suite # 1280, New York, NY 10010-3657

Copyright © 2011 by Windmill Books, LLC

CREDITS:
Author: Willow Clark
Edited by: Jennifer Way
Designed by: Brian Garvey

Photo Credits: Cover, pp. 4-5, 7, 9 (left), 10 (top, bottom), 17, 18, 20, 22 (top) Shutterstock.com; Cover (background) © www.iStockphoto.com/Shannon Keegan; p. 4 (inset) © Hecker/Sauer/age fotostock; p. 6 © www.iStockphoto.com/Rebecca Bagdanoff; p. 8 © Reinhard Dirscherl/age fotostock; p 9 (right) © www.iStockphoto.com/Neil Bradfield; pp. 10-11 © www.iStockphoto.com/David L. Amsler; p. 12 © Sylvain Grandadam/age fotostock; p. 13 © Jochen Tack/age fotostock; pp. 14-15 Jonathan and Angela Scott/Getty Images; pp. 16, 22 (bottom) Heinrich van den Berg/Getty Images; p. 19 (top) © www.iStockphoto.com/Klaas Lingbeek- van Kranen; p. 19 (bottom) © www.iStockphoto.com/Dave Rodriguez; p. 21 © www.iStockphoto.com/Stacey Lynn Payne.

Library of Congress Cataloging-in-Publication Data

Clark, Willow.
 Crocodile! / by Willow Clark.
    p. cm. — (Animal danger zone)
 Includes index.
 ISBN 978-1-60754-956-7 (library binding) — ISBN 978-1-60754-962-8 (pbk.) — ISBN 978-1-60754-963-5 (6-pack)
 1. Crocodiles—Juvenile literature. I. Title.
 QL666.C925C537 2010
 597.98'2—dc22

2010004430

Manufactured in the United States of America

For more great fiction and nonfiction, go to windmillbooks.com.

CPSIA Compliance Information: Batch #S10W: For further information contact Windmill Books, New York, New York at 1-866-478-0556.

TABLE OF CONTENTS

Big, Old Reptiles.................................... 4

Man-Eater?... 12

Baby Crocodiles.................................18

Did You Know?...............................22

Glossary...23

Read More....................................... 24

Index.. 24

Web Sites... 24

Big, Old Reptiles

Crocodiles are large **reptiles**. There are about one dozen kinds of crocodiles in the world. They can be found in the warm, wet parts of Africa, Asia, Australia, North America, and South America.

Scientists have found the bones of crocodile relatives that lived at the same time that dinosaurs lived on Earth.

Crocodiles are one of the oldest kinds of animals in the world. Scientists think crocodiles or crocodile-like animals have been around for about 200 million years. That means that crocodiles or their relatives have been around since the time of the dinosaurs!

Can you tell a crocodile apart from an alligator? These two animals are distant relatives of one another. It can be hard to tell them apart unless you know where to look.

Crocodile

Look at the animal's lower front teeth. If its mouth is closed and you can still see some of its lower teeth, it's a crocodile. Both animals have a terrible bite, so don't get close to either one!

Alligator

You can tell a crocodile from an alligator by looking at its lower teeth. Another difference is that crocodiles have narrower snouts than alligators.

Australia's saltwater crocodile can weigh up to 2,200 pounds (998 kg)!

How big are crocodiles? American crocodiles can grow to 15 feet (5 m) long. The largest crocodile is Australia's saltwater crocodile. It can grow up to 23 feet (7 m)!

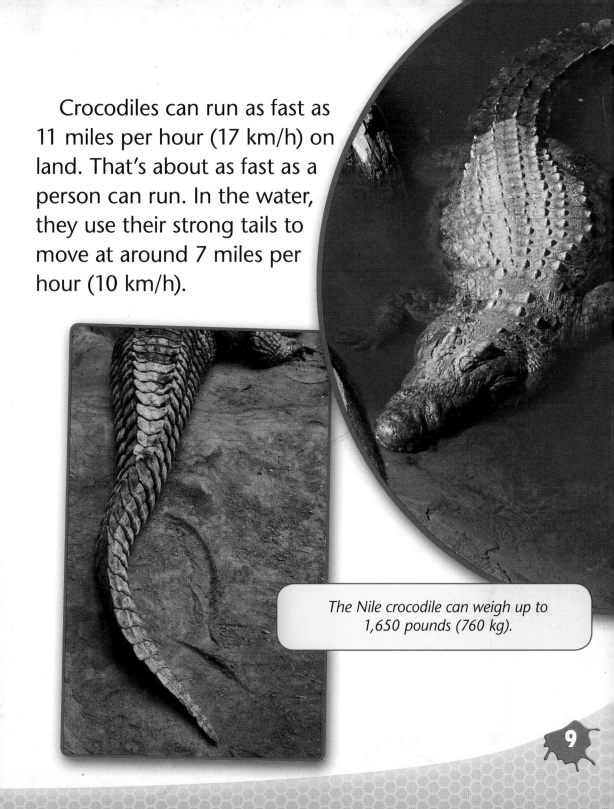

Crocodiles can run as fast as 11 miles per hour (17 km/h) on land. That's about as fast as a person can run. In the water, they use their strong tails to move at around 7 miles per hour (10 km/h).

The Nile crocodile can weigh up to 1,650 pounds (760 kg).

Crocodiles eat fish, crabs, turtles, snakes, birds, and small **mammals**. Nile crocodiles will eat bigger animals, such as hyenas, baboons, and lions.

Hyena

Baboon

Crocodiles are sneaky hunters. They float underwater near land. They wait for an animal to come to the water's edge for a drink. Then the crocodile leaps out of the water and grabs the animal in its mouth and drags it underwater. It holds the animal underwater until the animal drowns, then eats it.

A crocodile will eat just about anything that comes its way. Its strong jaws help it catch and kill its food.

Man-Eater?

Crocodiles are sometimes called "man-eaters" because they have **attacked** and killed people. The Nile crocodile alone is believed to kill about 200 people each year!

People who live near a crocodile's habitat need to look out for crocodiles that might be hunting for their next meal.

Although crocodiles try to stay away from people, people often live close to the crocodile's **habitat**. This makes it more likely that a person will come across a crocodile that is hunting. And because crocodiles aren't picky eaters, an unlucky person can easily become a crocodile's dinner.

JABIRU TOWN COUNCIL

NORTHERN TERRITORY

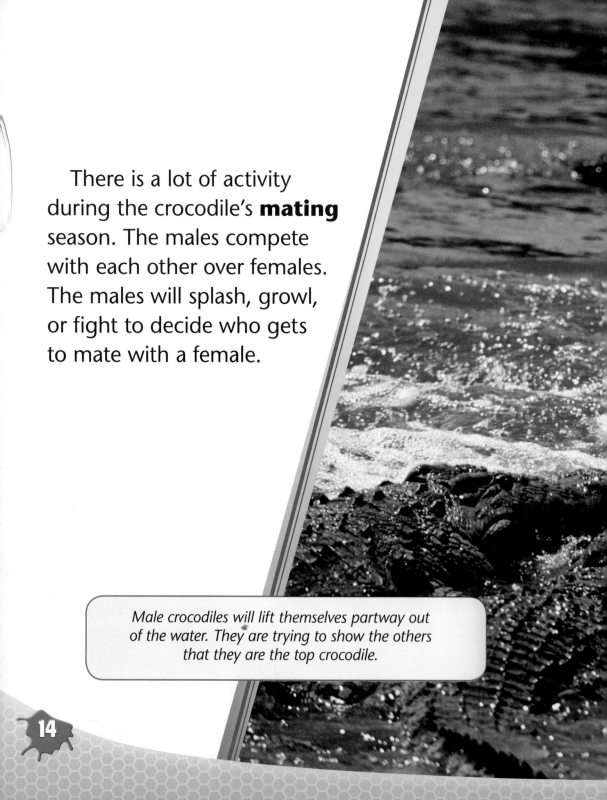

There is a lot of activity during the crocodile's **mating** season. The males compete with each other over females. The males will splash, growl, or fight to decide who gets to mate with a female.

Male crocodiles will lift themselves partway out of the water. They are trying to show the others that they are the top crocodile.

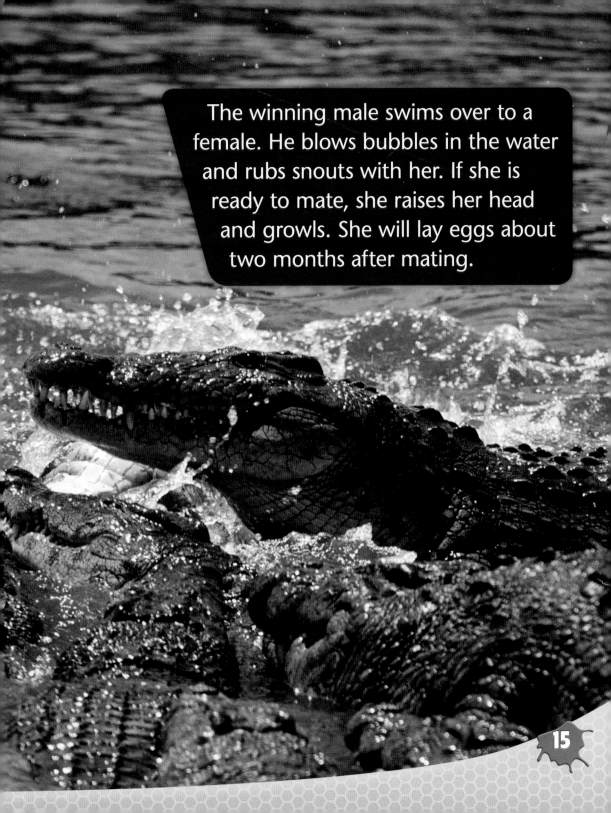

The winning male swims over to a female. He blows bubbles in the water and rubs snouts with her. If she is ready to mate, she raises her head and growls. She will lay eggs about two months after mating.

Crocodile eggs hatch about three months after they are laid.

When the female crocodile is ready to lay her eggs, she digs a nest for them and buries the eggs in it. The nests are often dug into riverbanks or dry streambeds. She will lay anywhere from 25 to 80 eggs in this nest.

The female crocodile only leaves her nest to eat and drink. She must guard her eggs from animals that want to eat them, such as raccoons.

Raccoon

Baby Crocodiles

When the eggs are about to **hatch**, the baby crocodiles make squeaky sounds. This tells the mother that it's time to dig up the eggs. Once the eggs have hatched, the mother guides her babies to the water for their first swim.

Young crocodiles live with their mother for up to two years. Very few baby crocodiles make it to adulthood. Most are eaten by other animals, even other crocodiles!

A baby crocodile is about 12 inches (31 cm) long. They grow at a rate of about 12 inches (31 cm) per year until they are fully grown.

Some **species** of crocodiles are **endangered**. That means they are in danger of dying out forever. Crocodiles are hunted for their skin, which is used to make leather goods.

Crocodile skin is used to make leather goods.

Dams can change the way a river flows. Changes in the water like this have an effect on the crocodile's habitat.

Crocodiles also suffer from habitat loss. This can happen when people build near where crocodiles live. There have been laws passed that are meant to protect the crocodiles from habitat loss and hunters. These laws have made it so that some crocodile species are no longer endangered.

21

Did You Know?

The word *crocodile* comes from the ancient Greek word for "lizard."

A crocodile can eat up to half its body weight in a single meal!

A group of crocodiles is called a bask.

Newly hatched crocodiles are called hatchlings.

The Nile crocodile lives for about 45 years in the wild. In a zoo, it can live as long as 80 years!

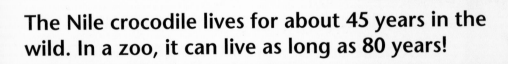

GLOSSARY

attacked (uh-TAKT) To have started a fight with.

endangered (in-DAYN-jerd) In danger of no longer living.

habitat (HA-beh-tat) The kind of land where an animal or a plant naturally lives.

hatched (HACHT) To have come out of an egg.

mammals (MA-mulz) Warm-blooded animals that have a backbone and hair, breathe air, and feed milk to their young.

mating (MAYT-ing) Coming together to make babies.

reptiles (REP-tylz) Cold-blooded animals with thin, dry pieces of skin called scales.

species (SPEE-sheez) One kind of living thing. All people are one species.

INDEX

A

alligator......... 6,7

American
crocodile.......... ...8

Australian saltwater
crocodile.......... ...8

B

babies.......... 18, 19

E

eggs 15, 16, 17, 18

H

habitat....12, 13, 21

M

mating...........14, 15

N

Nile crocodile...... 9,
..............10, 12, 22

READ MORE

Berger, Melvin. *Snap! A Book About Alligators And Crocodiles*. New York: Cartwheel, 2002.

Landau, Elaine. *Alligators and Crocodiles: Hunters of the Night*. New York: Enslow Elementary, 2007.

Pringle, Laurence. *Alligators and Crocodiles!: Strange and Wonderful*. Honesdale, PA: Boyds Mills Press, 2009.

WEB SITES

For Web resources related to the subject of this book, go to: www.windmillbooks.com/weblinks and select this book's title.